THE LIGHT CHANGES

THE LIGHT CHANGES

Amy Billone

Hope Street Press
Knoxville, TN 2013

ACKNOWLEDGMENTS

Grateful acknowledgment is made to the following publications in whose pages versions of poems in this book have appeared or else are forthcoming:

Ardent! Poetry in the Arts: "Third Trimester"
Barbaric Yawp: "Fox News"
Bellingham Review Online: "Long after Dark"
Blue Fifth Review: "Elegy for Jack Gilbert (1925-2012)"
Blue Lake Review: "Death Valley," "In This Age of War"
California Quarterly: "Cupid"
Chiron Review: "How Glorious It Feels," "Insomnia," "The Gift," "The Gun Salesman Said"
Connecticut River Review: "The Stars Said"
Haight Ashbury Literary Journal: "The Flight Attendant Said"
Hiram Poetry Review: "Why I Did Not Stay to See"
Knoxville Bound: "Reading *Mrs. Dalloway* at Junior's Diner"
MÖBIUS, The Poetry Magazine: "Invitation to a Carnival after a Storm," "The Poet Said" ("I want/to stretch the")
New Millennium Writings: "The Poet Said" ("The gold is right here")
Outscape: Writings on Fences and Frontiers: "First Trimester"
Pennsylvania English: "Intensive Care," "One Window Lit"
Plainsongs: "Grace"
Red Rock Review: "If Nothing Else"
Small Brushes: "But"
Still: The Journal: "First Job"
Wavelength: Poems in Prose and Verse: "The Cinnamon Maker," "The Poet Said" ("See:/as sudden")

Cover Art: Starling Flox (2005), watercolor painting by Maria Klawe

ISBN 978-0-9890740-0-1
Copyright 2013 by Amy Billone
All Rights Reserved
Printed and bound in the United States of America

In Memory of Jack Gilbert (1925-2012)

It was odd, she thought, how if one was alone, one leant to inanimate things; trees, streams, flowers; felt they expressed one; felt they became one; felt they knew one, in a sense were one; felt an irrational tenderness thus (she looked at that long steady light) as for oneself.

—Virginia Woolf, *To The Lighthouse*

With stammering lips and insufficient sound
I strive and struggle to deliver right
The music of my nature, day and night
With dream and thought and feeling interwound
And only answering all the senses round
With octaves of a mystic depth and height
Which step out grandly to the infinite
From the dark edges of the sensual ground.
This song of soul I struggle to outbear
Through portals of the sense, sublime and whole,
And utter all myself into the air:
But if I did it,—as the thunder-roll
Breaks its own cloud, my flesh would perish there,
Before that dread apocalypse of soul.

—EBB, "The Soul's Expression"

CONTENTS

PART 1   THE POET SAID

First Words	13
Grace	14
Enchantment	15
My Father Said	16
Fox News	19
Long after Dark	20
One Window Lit	21
After	22
First Step Out	23
First Job	24
The Poet Said	25

PART 2   THE GIFT

But	29
The Cinnamon Maker	30
Cupid	31
End of Summer	32
Mrs. Dalloway	33
The Poet Said	34
The Light Changes	35
Death Valley	36
The Gun Salesman Said	37
The Taste of It	38
The Gift	40

PART 3   FIRST TRIMESTER

Insomnia	43
Intensive Care	45
Email from my Father	46
The Flight Attendant Said	48
In this Age of War	49
Monet's Garden in Vétheuil	50
Paris to London	52
Why I did not Stay to See	54
Apology from my Father	55
Invitation to a Carnival	56
First Trimester	57

PART 4   IF NOTHING ELSE

How Glorious It Feels	61
Second Trimester	62
Elegy for Jack Gilbert	63
The Stars Said	65
Third Trimester	66
The Poet Said	67
Happy Endings	68
Tonight's News	69
Open the Door	70
First Breath	71
If Nothing Else	73

PART 1   THE POET SAID

FIRST WORDS

The same way at five I stared from the tub
into my father's terrified eyes after he broke
the bathroom door to save me because I hadn't
heard his calls and as he shook my body
to bring me back to life I laughed and told him
I didn't drown, the soap bubbles only filled my ears—
The same way at eight I looked into his gasping face
after he leapt from a moving car because I lay
sprawled on the grass by an upside-down bicycle
and as he lifted me with shaking arms I said I hadn't
fallen but was writing a poem about how the clouds
were really cotton candy—The same way
at sixteen I crashed my car into a street light
and fainted on the hardware store floor, then woke
to see him gazing blankly at me from the doorway
too frightened to remember the name
of my hospital so I said it for him—The same way
in my twenties I regained consciousness
after a six and a half day coma because I jumped
in front of a train I was so surprised to recognize
my pale-cheeked father waiting like a marble statue
by my side when we rarely talked and he lived
in a distant city that I spoke my first words
even though doctors had said if I survived
I would never recover language: *Hi Dad.*

GRACE

I was raped by a speeding train. I asked it to.

I threw myself before it. I extended my legs, arms.
It came when I called it. Oh what enormous

metal thighs. Oh what fast thudding hips. Again

again against my blackening eyes, skull, chest, waist—
I loved its greasy sighs. I loved its wild blows.

My mind flew away. Who pulled me from below?

Who fed me with a tube? Who brought me
sunflowers? Who hummed me lullabies? Who

pardoned me? Who ripped my shame in two?

ENCHANTMENT

At nine, I tore blank paper from my notebook, lit it to build
a fire. Secretly, I dried my hair by the fireplace, and brushed it
for my father. I planned to cast a spell on him, to make him
call me *Sweetheart*. He'd touch my yellow skull—*Sweetheart*,
he'd say, *Sweetheart*. Instead, he growled without lifting his eyes— *I
won't kiss you—You made your sister cry.* Eight years later, he was
the guilty one. She screamed that he had beaten her, drugged her
juice with Thorazine. Tied in bed at the asylum, she shouted *I'm not
crazy—I'm just mad*. Soon, her words became my own. The same
bed. The same chains. The same gown. Smoldering golden fur. My
bruises sparkle bluish purple where the fire's brilliance dies. *Daddy*.
Carry me on your shoulders, strong hands on my thighs.
Say I was born from your head like Athena. *Sweetheart*, say
Sweetheart— Kiss my cheek, my lips, touch my faded curls—Black
and blacker by the flames. Rub my back in circles, sing
Cockles and Mussels until I fall asleep—Drown me in a terrible
rainstorm, your fists lightning bolts, your voice thunder,
and all the stars in tears! I have no more blank paper.

MY FATHER SAID

I was 56 at the time.

Questions and Hypotheses

Facts are difficult to gather
and are generally incomplete. At best,
clues must lead to the most
probable root cause for the event.

    1. *How Did She End up on Her Back at the End of the Second Train Car under the Air Conditioner Unit with Her Feet Forward?*

Hypothesis A: She tripped onto the tracks.
Hypothesis B: She fainted and/or fell onto the tracks.
Hypothesis C: She was pushed off the platform.
Hypothesis D: She jumped.

If D is most probable, then question becomes
"Who was she?"

    2. *Introduction*

Phone call from detective. Accident,
critical condition, operating on her now,
cat scan, Trauma Center, fly there, hurry.

    3. *Retracing Steps*

Wait for train to approach and pass.

No room between train and wall for body.
Had to land and stop between tracks and ties.

Calculate downward distance from platform
edge to base of tracks (about 6 feet). Free
fall due to swooning would cause impact

with first rail at—Gravitational constant g
= 32.2 ft/s/s and terminal velocity
is square root of 2 times g times distance =
About 20 ft/s; But collision of body with first
rail would be inelastic—Not much bounce
upward; Maybe flipped and rolled into "coffin
space" between rails and ties—Minimum
energy state—Was there time to fall, hit, flip
and roll?—Possible, but not probable, but
still possible—How much time between fall
and train?—Wait for next train to stop.

She must have been standing here. She was
either pushed or she leapt. Momentum would
cause her to land directly between the rails.

Train could have passed right over her small body.
Mud and water and garbage between rails and ties
would cushion her impact to minimize bounce
and roll. That's how the first car passed over her
and she ended up under the second. But ran out
of clearance at end of second car. Most probable
conclusion: Pushed or jumped just before
train arrived at station, but inconclusive.

4. *Need to Talk to Detective*

What did the conductor see? *She flew
in front of train.* Were there witnesses?
Yes, one witness. What did he see?
He saw her jump. Why is case still open?
Witness may have pushed her.

Off the record, what do you think?
She jumped.

5. *Need to Retrace Her Thoughts*

Visit Apt. 5G; Search for diaries and notebooks.
Find notebook in which script progresses from

scrawl to chicken scratches. Conclude she was
not in her right mind; Not in her left mind.

Conclusion

On September 23rd, a girl jumped in front of a train.

The body of the girl belonged to my daughter.
The mind of the girl was a distorted version of
the mind of my daughter. But the heart and soul
of the girl did not belong to my daughter.

FOX NEWS

Tis the Season—Retailers Report
Christmas Sales Down—Too Many
Silent Cash Registers—So Why
Were All the Parking Lots Full?
—Cloning Controversy—Meanwhile
Lawyers Try New Ploy—Action
Quashed on 1st Amendment Grounds—
Fox News—New Baby on the Way—
Love Sick Boat—75 Passengers
Removed from Cruise Ship
In Key West Florida—The Ghost
Of Christmas Past—Thousands
To View Annual Dropping
Of the Ball—Guests will Include
The Mayor—Fox News—The Network
America Trusts—First Human
Cloned Today—Fox News—
20 to be Implanted in January—
Tis the Season—Fox News—
More than 18 Million Nationwide
Observe Kwanzaa—Swahili for
Fruit of the Harvest—Fox News—
Terror Strike—2 Powerful Bombs
Have Rocked the Capital—Cloning
Claims Fair and Balanced News—
Mayor Removed—Tis the Season—
Fox News—All Retailers Lawyers
Passengers Guests—Dropping of—
Nationwide Terror—Thousands
Of Bombs—18 Million Sick—
America Quashed—The Ghost
Of—Fox News—Fox News—

LONG AFTER DARK

My mind is probably going. I want
I want I want I want—Oh Dad, my mind
is in boxes. My mind is in boxes.

Dad, my mind is in boxes. My mind,
oh Dad—When the river speaks it says
nothing is really safe for me anymore.

I saw friends, I saw friends, I saw
them, I saw—What made the story run?
What made the song sung?

Dad, my mind is in boxes. My mind is
in boxes. My mind is in boxes, my
mind. First sleep came or tried to come.

ONE WINDOW LIT

Calm sea waves all night—Elevators up
and down, the falling of my head tipped plants—

I view their broken ribs, sunflowers' thick
bones turning over skulls, bells, orange lights

on trees. Today loved ones touch my bending face—
They cradle my weak trembling waist. I need

to stay awhile—Paper birds sway, leaves plead,
cathedral stained glass doors reach out and shut

like hands. In silence I watch winter's fist
grow tighter and unclench. It makes me sad

to see the whiteness of this writing desk—
My room, unheated, with one window lit.

AFTER

Miles and miles and miles and
miles—Focus—Am I still beneath
the train? All I recall is
death to hide death to hide
the shame in my eyelashes
the glue in my mouth too much
desire my quick thick heart—
Focus—Is this heaven?
Hundreds of bees, my head
cluttered with wings, vanishing
trees rats garbage growling
metal muscles, my bed
has weak sleepy feet. Huge
men push me upstairs downstairs
through hallways into blue rooms.
Voices cries needles tubes
screams. Someone is laughing.
Everyone weeps. I am terrified.
Focus. Blink back the disgrace.
For how many days and nights
has no one except the cathedral
out the window viewed the teeth
in my fists, my hungry heartbeat—
When will I stain these clean
sheets as well as the stormy sea
with endless blood from my fingers?
After miles and miles and miles and
miles—Come sit gently next to me.

FIRST STEP OUT

I wore a large green
straw hat my parents

bought to hide

the hole in my skull
Mom held

my left hand

Dad held my right
the busy city

a trampoline

I don't remember
clouds

FIRST JOB

Sunlight carves into my unused
desk and chair. On my empty
book shelf, a small bronze statue
curves his vigorous, muscled
spine, one elbow resting on a thick,
creased leg, a huge godlike fist under
his brooding chin. (Cathedral bells
chime seven times.) Behind him,
a woman's shadow looms featureless
in a Picasso print. She sits with her
head pressed to arms pressed to
knees. Maybe she is crying.
Right now I see her more easily
than the graspable, athletic,
thinking man. She seems more
solid than the setting sun's blonde
bands. This scares me. Tomorrow
I must bring my biggest books in.

THE POET SAID

See:
as sudden as
brushing arms
hot cheeks
goose bumps
touching lips
loosened knots
your legs on mine
the first time we
siren moans
praying hands
barking dogs
cries for help
rescuing feet
fireflies
homeruns
your waking eyes
my heartbeat

PART 2   THE GIFT

BUT

time
and tiny words
carved by
child hands
in tearing
bark of
expanding
garden trees
sawed down
by bare
gigantic
father arms
overwhelming

THE CINAMMON MAKER

Father, when you asked what I would become,
the answer felt too simple to explain:
A *Cinnamon Maker*, I always said. You sat
with Mom on a bench in the grass. Or beneath
a beach umbrella. In shorts or jeans or a summer
dress, I crouched digging until the deep sand caught
between my nails and skin. You both spoke, laughed,
but saw nothing. Day after day, by the shifting river,
I dropped wet sand from my left hand, dry sand
from my right. I wanted to create that twilight
spice forever, as delicious as cotton candy,
brown sugar, the thrill of something curious,
unexpected. Tell me, if today, too, I changed
the world as I did then, if I made this known to you,
might you at last reach toward the earth I have never
stopped shaping—Touch it—so startling, true?

C
   U
      P
         I
            D

> I
> only
> have this
> triangle to say
> everything inside: I
> ache to invade your heart

END OF SUMMER

I have a mind that glistensglares
I have a mind that cartwheelsspins
IhaveaIhaveaIhave a mind
that stuttersstumbling
but whirlwinding gathers speed
this mind reachesforyou wanting
this mind whispers to youbeckoning
this mind longs for you to
seeme knowme touchme
I have a mind that yearns for
yoursoftskin youreyelashes
yourhands in my hair
I have a mind that pleadsfor
forgiveness oh suffering
I have a mind thatoverflows
my body can't contain it
I sit still I go nowhere
I do nothing birdssweetlychatter
green leaves rise and dip
this sun is relentless
these fragrant houses
safeandyellow with porch
swings and lavenderflowers
I have a mind that behind
my scarred head
trainrumblesbreathlessly
it is hot summer the glittering river
waits for me mymindthismind
I have a I haveaI havea mind oh so
many turning bells and joltingwonders
what will I be and become

READING *MRS. DALLOWAY*
AT JUNIOR'S DINER

Last night, I dreamt I cooked the kitten in the oven. Next,
I bought a picture for my office. Three women in the dark. One
young and wealthy, one ancient and poor, one mad, lips open,

eyes wild. Their clothing was red. The blackness was smoke. Oh,
but look at the tree with white flowers! That running girl.

Her perfect muscles, her soft yellow curls. Today I watch a toothless
woman drink mashed potatoes mixed with milk through a straw.
Old men play pinball. I am no longer young. Remember the birches,

leafless, flinging their tired arms toward the river as our canoe
sailed past? They bent down, threw their necks backwards. And

Virginia. She drowned herself in the river. Leonard found her
walking stick but not her hat. She wore thick shoes that she hated.
In her pocket, a heavy stone. Afterwards, he stayed in the house

alone. All of her clothes, her unfinished knitting. Once, the voices
sped so fast, she heard sparrows singing in Greek. Everyone said

she was beautiful. Lovelier with age. And yet. The voices raced
ahead. Three girls in matching pink dresses dance by their table.
Her cheekbones are rose, the jogger. She wears a white sleeveless

shirt. White shorts. The tree. Mourning doves on the telephone wire.
My father's favorite photograph: Mother, Sister and me in red

jackets by the river. We children were tiny. Mother had black hair.
The waitress drops a plate. As I slept, the revelation: these women
are one person. But the bottom of the ocean. A walking stick.

The three pink girls twirl faster, faster. *Fear no more*, she repeated,
Fear no more the heat of the sun. Her body never reached the sea.

THE POET SAID

I want
to stretch the

reassurance but

you will not
have any guides.

The blind deaf
world is eating
itself alive.

Yet vividness is
unendurably
clear. The gratitude

of objects forces
non-existent
pictures to speak.

Love inanimate
beings as though
you gave birth

to them. No,
they are not true.

But everything
depends on you.

THE LIGHT CHANGES

The pain I know
doesn't.

Ugliness becomes
beauty, my mouth says.

My thoughts won't
unclear.

I'll jump from
a roof, put a gun

to my head. No,
my mouth says.

The gray light changes
will change

is changing now
as it always does.

You keep forgetting.
Stop.

DEATH VALLEY

It never rains here, my driver said. But
water was blinding; between rock sliding cliffs

stones sprang past the windshield.
I wanted to wreck the car, to drown.

This isn't sea level; it's Panamint,
he said. *Further down*.

My hand out the window turned warm and dry.
Lightning leapt behind huge mountains.

From Badwater, the lowest point
in the Western Hemisphere, to the top

of Telescope Peak, stretched eleven thousand feet.
In the darkness, he touched Trumpet shrubs

and carcasses of shrubs—Bones
overturned, thrown.

*Animals here are nocturnal;
they don't drink at all*.

Subdued now, dreading now.
Let's leave, I said. But he bent over

uprooted arms curved over heads,
bodies tossed, and hot, tipping half lives.

Water vanished in the air like smoke.
Time to go, he finally said.

But I kept waiting, my face poised,
motionless, above the ground.

So tired. So light.

THE GUN SALESMAN SAID

So you're here for the first time? You'll be glad
to know that women, after training, strike
the bull's eye more frequently than men. Once,
a lady fired at a life-size picture
of her husband she'd hung from the ceiling.
At last she shot the real guy in the chest
and herself, leaving their two kids behind.
Now I won't let you use detailed targets—
You've got to draw the line somewhere. For you,
I recommend a twenty-two light-weight
revolver. Go ahead, fill it up, push
the cylinder in place, step forward, bend
your knee, lean in, cock the gun, draw back, aim.
Keep in mind, if you flinch, I will smack you—
You need to press the trigger slowly—Then
you'll be surprised when the explosion comes.
Remember, if you blink, I will smack you,
I will smack you. That's right. Startle yourself.
Hit it—Surprise! Murder that hanging man—
Surprise! Again, again, with a tranquil
grip, burst open his stupid narrow heart.

THE TASTE OF IT

My purple eyelids,
purple lips and fallen hair,

this swollen tongue
and these limp fingers—

They will swim in you.

They are plums. They are melons.
They are necklaces and rings.

They are purple trees in autumn.
These, my words, are tumbling leaves.

Oh, the taste, the taste of it!

Berry berry violet sweet.
I have never been so giddy—

Lover in the darkness, put
your fist again against my cheek.

My face floats in a lilac ocean.

See how these eyes glitter—
Amethysts!

You sucked my breath
like helium. You squeezed

my hands around my throat.

Now you hover by my bedside,
wonder if I die or sleep.

But I throw glass slippers
in your ears, and bite your

knuckles—Huckleberries!

Oh, the taste, the taste of it!
I have never been so giddy—

Hear my teeth.
Hear my teeth.

THE GIFT

*You won't know which way
to hold it*, my father said,

his Christmas gift
a painted girl with felt eyes

and blonde yarn hair
on the back of an oval mirror.

But with shame and fear
as if from nakedness

I ran to the frozen river
covering her laughing mouth

with newspaper, snow,
branches, fragments of glass

not knowing that seven
months later a tan-armed boy

would say *Look, this washed up
in the sand*, how she would

startle me: a ghost child
with her smiling face

purple lips
and fading yellow hair—

Green eyes
in my green eyes.

PART 3 FIRST TRIMESTER

INSOMNIA

Me my father shame of stems together.

       ***

The same handwriting. Same sleepless
eyes. Green. Never to touch lucky
exhausted nature. No answer.

       ***

My father worked all night at the table.
He drew graphs on green lined paper. I sat
at the other end doing homework
with pencil and calculator.

       ***

In my bedroom when I couldn't sleep
I went to him for help. He rubbed my back
and sang lullabies about dying women
with names like mine. Like his.

       ***

Me my father shame of stems together.

       ***

My heart broke when he left my room because
he thought I was no longer there. I pretended
I wasn't. I cried beneath closed eyes.
Alive alive oh.

       ***

Mother and Sister—Their noisy pleading
madness—And my father suddenly unable

to hush them—Restless Legs Syndrome.

       ***

Grown up, I leapt desperately under
a train so as to reach floating beaches.
But glowing youth healed waiting warm
soothing nothingness never appeared.

       ***

Me my father shame of stems together.

       ***

Now almost dead I wake to feel him stroke
my hand with his weary feet in buckets
full of ice and to hear myself beg him not
to let this world's green window close ever.

INTENSIVE CARE

The wind is angry, warning
careful, careful: look around.

Leaves tap like children skipping.
Men and women laugh, opening

doors. Engines pick up speed.
A distant roar, the interrupted

pulse of animal jumps, a fierce
blow of horn. Softer now like

horses running, rapid, far away.
My father's voice. The even

breathing of nearby cars in lanes.
Sirens cry and sing. The shriek

of train wheels ceasing: not now,
not now.

EMAIL FROM MY FATHER BEFORE HIS FORMAL PRESENTATION ABOUT IMPACT TESTING OF HIGH-BURNUP CLADDING AT A SYMPOSIUM IN STOCKHOLM

This will be
as incomprehensible
to you as poetry
is to me but—

There are no
failed experiments.

I knew the sample
broke at the top
because of the skid
marks left by the hose
clamps but I wanted
to prove this to myself so

I went to Ace Hardware
and bought 6-inch-long
pipes, 3/8-inch inner
diameter with threaded
screws on both ends,
end-fitting caps to screw
onto the pipes,
hose clamps to fit
around them just below
and above the screws.

I packed all my bags
and flew to Sweden,
assembled everything
in my hotel room.

Just as I knew
would happen
the whole sample

broke in the top
weld region—
Every time I smashed
the system onto
the cement floor—

What is the positive spin?
Even though the stick
failed at the top,
impacted the bottom
of the test chamber
and shattered,

it still survived.

This, I will tell
my colleagues,
is dramatic and
convincing.

THE FLIGHT ATTENDANT SAID

Are you writing a letter?
    Excuse me?
What does this letter say?
    I'm grading papers.
Who is your letter to?
    Virginia Woolf.
Who?
    Virginia Woolf.
I thought I saw the word suicide.
    She drowned herself.
What?
    She ended her life.
The newly-wed from Sweden?
    What happened?
She jumped out the emergency
exit and fell 2000 feet.
    Could you say that again?
One man tried to save her; he yelled
and yelled but no one seemed to hear.
    What did you say she did?
She just jumped.
    I don't understand.
No one does. What are you writing?
    Forty-four pieces about
    Virginia Woolf.
I thought I saw the word suicide.
    By sinking into a river.
What?
    She just jumped.
That's what I heard. She must have been
insane.
    I don't think these students care
    about their grades anyway.
They didn't before. But after last week
we've been trained to be suspicious.
    I can't hear you.
Please stay seated.
    What did you say?
We're going down.
    Down?
Down.
    Down.

IN THIS AGE OF WAR

With what shrieking hysteria we fly
to eyelash thin telephone wires where we

crouch frightened close together. Now every
spoken word trips between our listening hands

and feet. Now dead people's voices shudder
inside our grasping fingers, toes. Clutch them,

we clutch them, swing we swing; our eyes seal tight
with longing. Who knows the answers to our

questions? Sunlight leaks into growing seas
and fallen leaves from assaulted trees hide

the dreamlike all-protecting garden doors
we would give anything to fit inside.

MONET'S GARDEN IN VETHEUIL

      Tall sunflowers the height
of rooftops, wider than house windows,

point toward the path, centers black
midnights, red dawns and evenings,

surrounded by full, stretching noons.

A boy pauses with a wagon in shades
of sapphire and violet, waiting for a faceless

woman and child to descend
the countless stairs.

      A French mathematician, interested
in African art, lives in the house now.

He shows me statues of Mwana Pwo,
beautiful maiden, her enormous eyes

closed, long lids pulled straight, dense lipped
mouth open over rows of many teeth, her high
forehead with marriage marks carved in.

      His funeral masks

are janus males and females, looking
forward and looking back,

some with immense circular eyeballs blasted wide
as if in shock, framed by thick light rims.

      Outside there is no garden anymore

only some tulips, a tree with no fruit,
an empty lawn,

but unobserved by the featureless people
on the stairs, the boy who looks into
the viewer's face, and blossoms with heads
up and back or at the ground

is the Seine

as though Monet drew it in the sky,
narrow, fluid, with hints of olive.

It rises secretly through the dissolving
houses in traces of blue—

Blue across the flower pots, the boy's clothes,
and those of woman and child, blue and white,
the indigo shadows on the path, the tops

of flowers, turquoise and plum.

He might have seen unnoticed rivers, too,
in the curving bodies of ancestors who spin

webs that serve as bridges, divination figures
holding liquid breasts, whirling heads

and shapes of dancers. And in the Nigerian

wooden face with pointed teeth larger
than eyes who speaks and reveals

the names of wrongdoers—

So strong that when he cries, tears burn into
his face, leaving furious clean white lines.

PARIS TO LONDON

Before the train
plunges into the sea,
I watch grazing deer
and horses sprinting,
green grape vines
and high corn leaves,
skinny full grown
leaning trees beside
baby saplings cradled
in nets, fields of
wheat, scattered rolls
of hay, an ancient
cathedral tower.
French students
smile, shout.
They must have lived
for thirteen years—
In their voices,
such wild joy.
I am sad to hear it.
They laugh together,
beautiful, young.
(We pass another
cathedral tower).
The children practice
English: *I love you, but...*
*one day...*a boy says
and a girl mimics him,
giggling. Others
repeat: *I love you, but...*
*one day...*They laugh
until their bodies shake.
I see no people outside
for hours. Only a solitary
man, bald-headed
like my father, leans
shirtless over blades

of grass. He must be
far away from home.
Then dancing sheep
and goats and purple
flowers. More youthful
laughter: *I love you, but...
one day*...My strange
familiar grief,
and still another old
cathedral tower.

WHY I DID NOT STAY TO SEE THE SECOND HALF OF SHAKESPEARE'S HENRY V

Before the play, Harold Pinter proclaimed
the United States was the most dangerous
force in history because of football
and mass destruction—Arrogant, violent,
ignorant, cruel, the misleading media,
a madman elected illegally,
etcetera. The British cackled, clapped
hysterically. I clapped, too, worried that
I was starting to have my period.
The show was a satire of the war with
Iraq: dropping bodies, tanks, bombs and smoke.
I gasped for air and thought about my pants,
the bottom of my coat, the fancy chair.
How wetness might be seeping through my seat
and leaking to the floor. Between acts I
found a machine on the restroom wall but
even though I paid one pound I couldn't
find buttons to push or dials to turn.
I shook and shook the smooth white metal box.
At last I panicked, fled. Waterloo sells
wine, batteries, books, chocolate and clocks—
I went from shop to shop. One had brand new
adaptors beside toothbrushes, candy,
cigarettes, umbrellas. "Excuse me, Sir,
do you sell tampons?" "Yes, for what country?"
the salesman asked. "No, tampons," I said.
"I understand. We have them. For what code?"
"I don't know." "Buy this," he said,
and gave me an international telephone card.
I took the train and the blood kept flooding
everywhere—Through my face, down my legs,
between my toes. I covered my eyes.
How did I manage to do so much wrong?

APOLOGY FROM MY FATHER

I have written
three brilliant
replies to you.

All of them
failed to go
through

because
you and I
have used up

our away
from home
inferior sounds

and colors.
I will have to
download

my words
of wisdom
to you,

save them
as a word
document,

recompose
and resend.
I hope I can.

Maybe I will
tomorrow.

INVITATION FROM A CARNIVAL AFTER A STORM

When the hard rain started everyone fled
except for soccer-kicking boys who keep
collapsing in wet grass, an old wide eyed
barefooted woman with torn up pants, large
sores on her legs, a black hatted man hunched
on a bench over a black cloaked guitar,
drenched plastic curtains half whipped away
from empty stages where polka-dotted
horses fly frozen in mid air, and my
afraid body. I am not beautiful.
Still, my hands are gentle. My voice is soft.
No one sees me. I will always be here,
today, tomorrow, every day until
my death and after my death which happened
perhaps long ago, waiting for you, friend.

FIRST TRIMESTER

It all may come down in one way or another
to the two cats. A few weeks ago I called my gray
cat inside but at the last minute as I closed the door
another gray cat ran in, too. The collarless stray
has a chopped off tail. It cries all the time.
I let it out that night and it came back the next
morning. It haunts this house. My mother who
has an uncanny way of being right asked *What is
its gender? I think it's a boy*, I said. *The gender
of the cat is the gender of your unborn baby*,
she said. And his chopped off tail, his fragile body,
his ceaseless crying? But his kindness, too.
Today he ran eagerly toward me in the street.
The answers to my questions feel just out of reach.

PART 4   **IF NOTHING ELSE**

HOW GLORIOUS IT FEELS

      when you place
your terribly
      evaporated

      all relieving
heart blinking
      hands against

      this unseen
weeping face
      my god

SECOND TRIMESTER

Red numbers on the clock.
Changing, changing. The baby
pokes me from inside. Again,
I think, again, again. The sound
of a car, a train, nothing? Objects.
Their rude permanence.
Excitement. A symphony within me.
Three quick black birds. The joy
of them as they cut cut cut
the unrelenting sea gray sky.

ELEGY FOR JACK GILBERT (1925-2012)

It was a pretty day in May, 2004. He was working as Writer in
Residence at the university. We drank hot chocolate together at my
favorite cafe. I showed him folders full of poems I wrote called

"The Poet Said," each made up of notes I took during the lectures he
gave. I crushed my cake into many pieces with the side of my spoon.
He laughed and told me my food looked like it had been destroyed by

a bird or a raccoon. He explained how embarrassing it was to have
lost his memory. Those days, he couldn't find his office, his
apartment, his way when he went outside. He showed up late to

class or failed to come at all because he forgot the building where his
class was held. It was hard for him to speak and read. He no longer
remembered who his favorite poets were. He wouldn't say my name

but instead called me "the auditor"—he knew me as the professor
sitting in on his graduate class. But he still spoke about his past
with surprising specificity. I played with my cake and spilled

whipped cream on the table while he talked. He said the first time
he made love to a woman whose name we will always remember,
Michiko threw eggs into a pot and removed the broken shells with

her fingers. She stirred the eggs until they turned gray. Then she
leaned against the edge of his chair and breathed onto his neck
while he looked at her album of snapshots. Her hair on his throat

was so distracting he saw nothing as he studied page after page.
The last time he kissed her he was shocked her dead young skin
could be so cold. Now the world cannot forget Michiko's skin

was the color of pale honey; nor can we forget she had trouble
sleeping because of the sound of petals falling from the roses
he gave her. As we left the cafe he exclaimed how happy he felt

in the gentle Spring sun. But he also said the happiest he had ever
been was during his deepest grief for Michiko in the days and weeks
after she died. He had never felt more alive. When he stepped out of

my car he smiled and said he enjoyed talking with me because
I was so naked. I wondered if he'd remember our conversation.
Why am I ashamed to admit this? *I wanted him to know my name.*

THE STARS SAID

We were everywhere—
Physical nervous
ready yes yes—
The brain was
dreadfully pleased.
You couldn't count us.
Your eyes were
impossibly young.
Now your skin grows more
ancient than the moon.
Blackness hides us.
We laugh in all the trees.
But you are on the edge
of all you do not
know yet—
Believe this
or take your life:
We are brightening.

THIRD TRIMESTER

My God, I have never loved
anything as much as these
ripples inside me. This delicious
seaweed in the thirsty blue
water stretching itself every
which way. On the beach.
Friends. Hot sand. My skinny
arms and legs tan happy child
perfect. I feel that way today
although now I am unable even
to walk comfortably from here to
there. But I am changing
faster than I did then. So is he.
The boy inside me who likes
movies and late nights. We
will never be this close again.

THE POET SAID

The gold is right here.
You need to lift it up

because of the clock.
The stars and planets

don't know what season
it is. Loneliness is

astonishing. It will cost
you everything to do

what needs to be done.
Shouting isn't enough.

Forget nothing. Trees
are beautiful, those trees.

Years later, will you
remember how many

windows there are
in this room? Watch:

my black umbrella turns
into a smashed hollow

pumpkin when I open
it indoors. You must

bring it back to life for me.
Or else we're doomed.

HAPPY ENDINGS

A Nuclear Regulatory Commission research program on high-burnup nuclear fuel took a major step forward when a shipment of commercial spent fuel rods finally arrived after years in limbo. The shipment, which included two North Anna M5-clad high-burnup rods and two Robinson-2 Zircaloy-4-clad high-burnup rods, is a key element of NRC's program to more fully understand the impact of a loss-of-coolant accident or LOCA on high-burnup fuel, as well as how it will perform in a dry cask storage environment.
During a LOCA, fuel cladding is expected to heat up, balloon, pop, heat up further, then be quenched by the reactor's automated safety system. According to a famous Irradiation Performance Section Manager who recently returned from Stockholm, it has taken years to "re-establish the capabilities we lost." Perhaps happiness and truth will now be achieved in record time.

TONIGHT'S NEWS

If you look closely
in the hours before
sunrise, you might see

an illusory UFO
hovering above
the southwestern horizon.

In truth, you observe Venus,
the most luminous
she has been all year.

OPEN THE DOOR

Let the good news in.

He is struggling on the other side,
      denting the wood with his limbs,
saying *I'm ready I'm ready*.

Everyone is waiting. It will be
      hard. It will be explosive. Bombs
will go off, hurricanes, fireworks.

I'm longing for him.

FIRST BREATH

I.

The lovely clock—
Its red numbers
glittering blood
I can taste
as I bite my lip
and gaze out
the illuminated
window.

II.

The gray skied world
I see outside
seems to be
in a little pain.
No birds.
Some cars.
Slits between blinds
like opening skin.
Relax, nurse Jenny
says to me.
Don't fight the shakes.
Give in to them.

III.

Fast. Must go faster.
Hard. Must push harder.
Look at the baby's head
in the mirror,
Dr. Briscoe says.
It can be a focal point.

Instead, I think of
how paramedics
pulled me from below,
Dr. Stephen drained
my bleeding brain,
friends brought me
sunflowers,
Father sang me
lullabies,
Mother and Sister
wept and kissed me,
telling me my name
and age, where
I was born,
what my childhood
had been like.
It was a miracle case.

*This is the most
important thing
you will ever do,*
Jenny shouts.
Give it all you've got.

IF NOTHING ELSE

If nothing else let me point to that tree
full of loud starlings in the evening cool.
How quickly it's darkening. The breeze grows.
The birds sit so close their bodies touch. See
how they balance and swing. What a wild thrill
of urgent highs, lows and fluid lovely tunes!
Huge flocks arrive, responding to these calls.
The branches look ready to break—Then all
at once, not slowly fading, but instead
suddenly ceasing, the feverish shouts die,
the breathless pausing birds lift their gorgeous
exploding voiceless wings, the leafless oak
bursts in silent fireworks (my heart) and sparks
fly to the river in the falling crimson night.

ABOUT THE AUTHOR

AMY BILLONE has published poems widely. Her academic book *Little Songs: Women, Silence, and the Nineteenth-Century Sonnet* (Ohio State University Press, 2007) is the only extended study that has been written about nineteenth-century female sonneteers. *Little Songs* offers a complex analysis of the overwhelming impact that silence makes, not only on British women's poetry, but also on the development of modern poetry and thought. Billone wrote the Introduction and Notes for the Barnes and Noble Classics edition of *Peter Pan* (2005). She is an Associate Professor of English at the University of Tennessee, Knoxville. She holds a Ph.D. in Comparative Literature from Princeton University. Her scholarly and creative work appears in major academic and literary journals. She lives with her two sons in Knoxville, Tennessee.

ABOUT THE ARTIST (STARLING FLOX, 2005)

MARIA KLAWE is a renowned computer scientist and mathematician and the first female president of Harvey Mudd College. Prior to leading HMC, she served as dean of engineering and professor of computer science at Princeton University. Klawe has made significant research contributions in several areas of mathematics and computer science, including discrete mathematics, human-computer interaction, gender issues in information technology and interactive-multimedia for mathematics education. Klawe is also an artist and has painted throughout her academic career. She finds math, science and engineering to be highly creative disciplines and enjoys seeing scientists' creative energy, passion and talent cross into the arts.

www.ingramcontent.com/pod-product-compliance
Lightning Source LLC
LaVergne TN
LVHW041635070426
835507LV00008B/648